GOD
Was Holding My Hand

GOD
Was Holding My Hand

Michael
Arterberry's
Story

WRITTEN BY

RACHEL ARTERBERRY

Inspiring Voices®
A Service of **Guideposts**

Inspiring Voices books may be ordered through booksellers or by contacting:

Inspiring Voices
1663 Liberty Drive
Bloomington, IN 47403
www.inspiringvoices.com
1-(866) 697-5313

ISBN: 978-1-4624-0405-6 (e)
ISBN: 978-1-4624-0406-3 (sc)

Library of Congress Control Number: 2012920812

Printed in the United States of America

Inspiring Voices rev. date: 11/16/2012

Each person is given something to do that shows who God is: Everyone gets in on it, everyone benefits. All kinds of things are handed out by the Spirit, and to all kinds of people!

1 CORINTHIANS 12: 7

Contents

The BIG Wake up   9

Metamorphosis   11

A New Beginning   15

Walking like Jesus   19

Forging a New Path   23

Buckle Up!   29

Why Me?   35

Update   55

H AVE YOU EVER HAD THE FEELING THAT GOD WAS WITH YOU, sitting there next to you? Walking with you? God has been with me my entire life...I just didn't know it.

It was not usual for women in the late 1960's to be having children at age thirty six, so, when my mother went to the doctor, she had already assumed she was going through early menopause. Little did she know God had already set a plan in motion for her to be my mother. Imagine her surprise when the doctor informed her that she was pregnant. I was born on January 5, 1968 and was named Michael, which means "gift from God". And so, the journey of my life began.

My mother, Lillie Ruth was born near Birmingham, Alabama and my father, O.B. was from Mississippi. Neither of them finished their education past the eleventh grade yet they were able to provide for their three children while living in Alabama. It was the 1960's and the world was a different place. It was a time when blacks and whites in the South did not mingle, having separate schools, water fountains and churches. My siblings clearly remember the Sixteenth Street Baptist Church bombing in Birmingham in 1963 and vividly recall how they were treated as black children growing up during these tumultuous times.

In July, 1965 my parents decided that to provide a better life for the family it was time to move to New York where my father had relatives. It seems to me that it was part of God's plan to have my parents and their three children, ages twelve, ten and eight, make this move. Coming to New York was a huge adjustment for everyone; schools were desegregated and society was more accepting and open to people of all races, colors and backgrounds. My father got a job as a bus driver and my mother became a housekeeper for several wealthy families.

If I were an outsider looking into the dynamics of my family at the time, I would see a hardworking, God-loving, close family. Everyone my father came into contact with simply adored him. He was generous, funny and always ready to have a good time. My friends all thought I had the coolest dad. They did not have a clue what was really going on in my house, the chaos that existed, and my shame. The rule in our house was that you did not put your dirty laundry on the street. No one knew that my father had become a verbally abusive alcoholic. Being twelve years younger than my closest sibling, I am always reminded that I grew up in a "different" house than they did. Dad liked to party hard and hang out late into the night. He would keep my brothers and sister up when they were teenagers and into their twenties so that they could all listen to music and hang out.

Me? I was a momma's boy, but I knew exactly how to get what I wanted. I would ask my mother for new sneakers, and when she said no, clearly because we couldn't afford it, I would go to my dad and he would demand she do it. I would jump in my mother's lap so he wouldn't scream at her, knowing I was listening.

As I got older I could hear the various patterns of my father's steps and know what to expect when he came through the door; a loud slam of the front door followed by delayed, erratic steps and a pause at the door to our apartment meant that he was drunk and trying to gather himself before entering. Quick steps on the stairs meant that he was sober and in a good mood. There was many a night when I would lay in my bed and listen for those steps to determine the mood of the house. I never feared that my father would physically hurt me, but I knew that the cut of his tongue was more severe than any physical abuse. As the youngest, I seem to have been least affected by his verbal lashings. This also made him very uninvolved in my life. In an unstable home like mine, you never knew what to expect.

Being raised in a Seventh Day Adventist Church, it was normal for my mother and me to attend church early on Saturday morning. This was my first experience with God, and from a young age, I knew that He loved me. What I didn't know was the plans that He had for my life and that He would be with me every step of the way. As I got older, I did not want to go to church on Saturdays; I wanted to play sports - soccer, football, basketball, baseball. Whatever the season, I wanted to play it. I told my father how I felt…and that was the end of my Saturday church attendance.

Fortunately, I was a talented athlete and quickly took to whatever sport I tried. At a young age, I started to be noticed by coaches. Athletics quickly became a diversion from what was going on at home and saved me from being consumed by it. But, I did not have the same experience that other kids had. I would watch parents at football games cheering for their kids and feel sad that mine weren't there. My mother was dedicated to worshipping God and would not allow my activities to interfere with that. It was her spiritual strength, commitment to God, and constant prayer that kept our family strong and united, although it was very difficult to understand at times. Between her trying to keep our family together and putting food on the table, my time with her was limited.

It became clear to me that I would need to rely on myself for encouragement and support during my sports activities without my family as my support system. Of course, they were proud when I came home with the MVP trophy from football or baseball or soccer or even the varsity letter as a sophomore in high school. I always knew that I was loved, but

4

we were not the type of family to hug and kiss and support one another like that. After I won my first MVP award, I was driven to do better. My competitive spirit kicked in, and I was constantly motivated to do more, to be better. I knew I would be getting that "extra" trophy on awards night, driving me to work harder during the season.

My coaches could sense that I did not have a role model at home, so they would try to take me under their wing. I thank all of them for their concern. God brought other male mentors into my life to help me excel during these difficult, impressionable years. Whether it was a concerned parent driving me home from soccer camp or a coach getting me into Little League before I was eligible, I had people there to encourage me to be all that I could be and keep my environment from me. Sports and mentors prevented me from becoming a victim of my community and the environment I lived in. Many of my childhood friends who did not have the same opportunities as me got caught up in drugs and crime.

As I got older, I became drawn to working with kids. At fifteen, I began working as a camp counselor at the local YMCA. As young as I was myself, I began to see that I had a way with kids. They seemed to like being around me, and I always connected with several of them during the summer. I vowed at that time that I would give back to the youth, knowing very well that without strong role models in my life, I could have ended up a drug addict or in prison.

Although I was feeling great helping kids who were younger than me, I still was experiencing challenges of my own. When I was in the eleventh grade, I was being recruited by some of the biggest schools in the nation for football. I had always had great athletic ability, but I was a very poor student. I dreamt of becoming a professional football player, like so many other young men. My teachers, family, and friends were all excited for the possible opportunity for me to get a scholarship to the school of my choice, with the hopes of then moving on to professional football. Thinking that a scholarship was in the bag, I had been doing the minimum in my classes. To my surprise and disappointment, the NCAA passed a rule called Proposition 48 requiring an SAT score of eight hundred and a C average in school. I lost all of the scholarships that were offered to me. What in the world would I do now? This was NOT part of my plan.

This was one more hardship that I had to experience at a young age. In December of my junior year, tragedy struck my already fragmented family. My father had passed out in a drunken stupor inside his old Cadillac, which was parked on some dried leaves. The leaves caught fire, igniting the entire vehicle. After spending several days in a burn unit my father died, leaving me shocked and yet conflicted. I missed him then because of the title that he had in my life but "dad" was not the imprint that he left on my life. I miss him today for the moments that I would like to share with him, and I wish he could see the man that I have become.

These two devastating events behind me, I decided to attend the local community college with a lesson that I vowed to share with any young person that would listen to me. Because of some poor decisions in my life, things were different than "I" had planned and different than those around me expected. What I could not see at the time was that my plan was not God's plan. It was not God's plan for me to become a professional athlete. If I had had my way, I am certain I would not be here now with this story.

I finally got my act together in community college and then transferred to Iona College where I fell into my gift, social work. Although I did not go to college necessarily to play football, I did play at both colleges. I still had a glimmer of hope of playing professionally one day until my dream was finally dashed completely. After breaking my ankle two years in a row, I concluded that my dream was over. My new goal was to obtain a degree I could use to work with the youth once I graduated. I did very well with my social work classes because I could relate. My life journey so far was similar to so many of the young people I would be working with.

While in college, I worked at a runaway shelter and a junior high school. Again I saw that there was something about my personality that made the youth feel comfortable around me. They would share intimate details about their lives and look for guidance. Teachers were impressed with how students behaved after working with me and complimented me on my work. I graduated from Iona College in 1991 with a Bachelor's Degree in Social Work. Since I was the first member of my family to graduate from college, naturally they were all extremely proud of me.

My first job out of college working with youth was with a foster care agency where my responsibilities included monitoring the care of the foster children in the foster home and building relationships with them to help them have a positive experience in the foster care system. I soon received a promotion and became an Independent Living Specialist, teaching boys living in group homes indispensable life and social skills as well as providing emotional support. The most important role that I had was helping the youth transition from the foster care system to living on their own as responsible adults. After several years, I decided to move on to another agency where I was a school counselor, designing service and support plans to meet the unique needs of the students under my supervision. Over the next several years, I worked with teens in many different capacities. I monitored teen-led community service projects. I supervised a bi-weekly radio broadcast program, and developed a youth forum within the community. All of these activities were in preparation for and leading up to my next big endeavor.

The BIG Wake up

IN EARLY 2001, all of my friends and I were getting ready to make the big jump into marriage. Well, really, the girlfriends were preparing, we were just going to show up. My longtime girlfriend, Rachel and I were so excited to be starting this part of our lives together. My best friend and his fiancé decided they were going to be water baptized in a Baptist church and give their lives to Christ before they got married.

As I sat there in the packed church service, watching them dedicate themselves to Jesus Christ and become saved, it happened. The Holy Spirit spoke to me and I just knew what I had to do. I had to be saved, born again. I gave my life to Christ right then and there and was forever changed. This was a new beginning for me. My journey towards what God had always planned for me was about to begin.

I had always believed in God. Even in my deepest, darkest years of partying and misbehaving, I knew that God was there for me and I never went to bed without saying the

Lord's Prayer. I had never been ready before to truly give my life to Him. This was one call that I could not ignore. I was not prepared for the amazing transformation that was about to take place.

Metamorphosis

YOU MAY BE FAMILIAR WITH THE CHILDREN'S STORY, "The Very Hungry Caterpillar" by Eric Carle. I was like the "hungry caterpillar", eager to eat as much food, spiritual food as I could. Looking back, this transition from a caterpillar, a baby Christian, to a beautiful butterfly was much more than a week of being "hungry" for the word of God. It was instead a very rough several years.

Because I had grown up in the church, I had an idea as to where to begin my journey. I went to see my spiritual guide, my praying mother. This was the beginning of a new relationship for her and me. We sat for hours on end talking about scripture and verse and what it all means. I decided it was time for a new "me". This meant discarding all of my former bad habits and destructive behavior; removing the flashy jewelry I had been wearing during my wild party days, and modifying my choices of music and movies. It was difficult to give up some of these things, but it was preparing me. It was a sign that what was coming was more than I could expect or was ready for. I prayed, but was I really praying? Or was I just going through the motions of something I had learned in Sabbath school as a kid? Did I really know how to talk with God and have a relationship with him? This amazing woman that prayed her children through school; prayed her youngest son through the wild years; prayed her grandchildren through rough times; she was there for me now as well to teach me how to pray and how to accept God's word and use it in every aspect of my life. Our relationship grew by leaps and bounds. She loved to cook the equivalent of a Thanksgiving dinner every time I stopped by simply to celebrate my visiting with her. It was a very special time in my life as I learned more about her and the amazing relationship that she had with God. I learned to be a praying man, preparing me for the rest of my life.

Rachel was having a very difficult time with my transformation. She liked the "Michael" she was getting ready to marry. She had grown up in a stable home. She went to church every Sunday, but there was no relationship with God. There was no praying to thank God for his goodness or to praise Him with song. She understood church and God to be a responsibility and nothing more. She had no desire to get closer to him and was very resistant to my doing so. We argued. It was very stressful because I knew in my heart that I was called to draw nearer to God yet my relationship with my soon to be wife was being stretched. Rachel could not understand why I would change my lifestyle for anyone let alone God. I dove into the Bible and read every Christian book I could get my hands on. This was very comical since Rachel had tried to get me to read for years, but I always insisted that I didn't like to read. Now here I was, ravenous to devour as much spiritual food as I could get. I was baptized in April 2001 and began my new life as a Christian. It was no coincidence that God placed the desire to be closer to Him in my friends' hearts first, but I believe that this calling was meant for me. It was part of His plan for my life.

Rachel and I were married on June 22, 2001. What an amazing day! Although we decided not to be married in a church, we did agree on a non-denominational minister to perform the ceremony. I knew all along that God was there with us orchestrating everything; from the ceremony to the reception to the smiles on our friends' and families' faces. He even had the sun come out for the outdoor service when clouds threatened that morning. If only Rachel could see it! For her, 'she' had done all of this; arranged for the perfect place, selected the best food and planned down to every last detail. I hoped that one day she would realize that although she physically made the plans, God made it all possible for us to start our new life together in such an amazing way.

A New Beginning

2001 WAS A VERY BUSY YEAR FOR US. I was saved, we were married, we bought our first home and Rachel started a new job. All the while, I was studying, reading, and learning the word of God. I decided to attend the Baptist church where I first felt led to God in Mount Vernon, NY. This church had special meaning to me and I enjoyed the service. The challenge was that we had moved to Danbury, Connecticut which was about an hour away. Rachel could not understand my newfound love for God or my desire to drive an hour each way to sit through service for several hours and then drive an hour home. "This was an all day affair for heavens sake"! So we argued! It wasn't long before I realized something had to change. I knew that if we were to have children, I would want to raise them in a Christian home. This meant a father and mother who loved and served the Lord. This was not going to happen unless something changed in one half of this equation. How could I get her to change? How would I be able to convince her that God had a plan for her life too and that she was not in control of 'everything' (as she thought)?

I talked and she blocked. I talked some more and she continued to block. Finally, for me, she considered attending a local church. I felt as if we had just made a giant leap. This was not going to be easy though. I was comfortable in my Baptist church with the amazing praise and worship team and the 'Yes' and 'Amen'. All Rachel knew was the obligatory sit, stand and kneel of a very traditional religious belief. We needed to find a church where we could both feel comfortable. God led us to a place called Bright Clouds, a small non-denominational church near our home. We had driven past several churches and peered inside. They just didn't have the allure to draw us in to actually attend service. Bright Clouds was different. The pastor was about our age and the sanctuary was a sea of diversity. I knew right away that this was where God wanted me to be. We were not the only bi-racial couple, in fact we did not stand out among the many different races of people there worshipping. Isn't that really the point? God didn't make us black or white or Italian or Asian? We are all children of God, no matter what we look like. This was a comfortable place for me. For Rachel, however, this was still a very foreign place. The church had a wonderful, upbeat praise and worship team. The pastor very simply showed how the Bible and its teachings apply to our lives and how God wants us to have a relationship with Him. He does not want us to only go to church and praise Him on Sundays alone.

We began to go regularly and to meet new people. I was fully committed to learning God's word; studying, changing my life and walking in my Christian path. Rachel continued to go to please me, but was not yet convinced that Jesus was her savior or that she even needed one in fact. I vividly recall her body language…crossed arms, sitting perfectly erect, determined not to let the word of God infiltrate her brain and her very being. Eventually her body gave in. Through their praise, the worship team convinced her limbs first that it was okay to express feelings. First it was a tap, then a wiggle. Her love to dance overcame her resistance to church and what it represented. I couldn't help but smile at her as she began to even sing. It brought such joy to my heart to see her slowly, very slowly opening up to the ideas that the pastor was sharing with us each week. All the while, I was desperate to receive as much of His word I could possibly get.

Walking like Jesus

I WAS A BABY CHRISTIAN and was eager to tell the world about what I had learned, how God was working in my life and how I was transformed. Unfortunately, the world that I was in was NOT ready to hear it. Friends that I grew up with, the ones that I partied with and relied upon, all thought I was crazy. They too could not understand why I was changing all of my worldly ways and giving up things that "I" had worked for just like they had. They did not understand what it meant to be walking with Jesus, salvation and doing things for others for His glory. How was I to convince them? Initially, I thought preaching was the way. I was so excited about what I was learning that I expected others to want to hear it too. I assumed that everyone should long to be closer to God, to walk with Jesus. Instead I received cold shoulders, fewer phone calls and less boys' nights out. I finally realized it could only be through my actions that they would see. What would Jesus do? Jesus would love everyone with no expectations for anything in return. He would share the Word through His actions. This is how I would live my life. I would be a blessing to everyone that I would come across in any way that I could. My friends used to call me paranoid during the wild days when we all threw caution to the wind. My paranoia was in fact, the Holy Spirit there with me, urging me to do what was right. After giving my life to Christ, the Holy Spirit's voice was the one that I was hearing and listening to.

The world is a very difficult place. God had now given me a gift to share His Word through my actions and it is my responsibility to do so. Although my father was not a believer and his actions were not representative of what I would call a good Christian, he did have some very good qualities about him. He was extremely generous to others. Whether it was providing a ride or giving his last dime, my dad always gave. He had no idea that he was sharing God's love. I had always followed in my father's footsteps in this way, but now I truly understood why. Youth that I worked with at the group homes experienced it; guys that I grew up with experienced it; strangers and friends experienced it. If someone needed five dollars, I gave them fifty. I was in the barber chair one day and saw a young woman come in, clearly hardened by the streets even in her young age. I quietly paid the barber for her haircut and walked out, not wanting her to know who had helped her. Several months later I learned that she passed away. I hope that for one small moment in her life she felt loved. A young man working at an auto repair shop, going through a divorce, sleeping on a friend's couch was shamefully telling me his story. I opened my wallet and gave him all that was in it. I have never done these things for recognition or praise but simply to show others the kindness and generosity of strangers and that God is always watching out for them. This is my responsibility as a Christ follower.

Forging a New Path

IF ONLY I HAD KNOWN THEN that what started out as a staff training day for work would change my life forever. My coworkers and I were less than enthusiastic about attending this mandatory training on our day off. Just to satisfy my training requirements, I registered for the only interesting course being offered, AVP (Alternatives to Violence Project).

When I entered the room, I immediately noticed the chairs were strangely arranged in a circle and everyone appeared to be a little anxious about what was going to happen. I was a little leery, but was willing to give it a chance. A young woman opened the session with some ice breakers to get us comfortable and then some interactive exercises to encourage us to work together. During one of these sessions, I had the opportunity to share my Christian Faith. As the day progressed, I could see my co-workers beginning to transform. The group had actually developed into a community. There was a lot of laughter, tears, and genuine compassion for each other. As I witnessed this amazing transformation, my brain went into overdrive. If these activities worked with a group of adults, social workers at that, imagine what it could do with kids? I needed to get this information, needed to learn more.

I approached the facilitator and expressed how truly impressed I was with the workshop. She mentioned to me that on the 'outside', AVP trainings occur only four times a year but, on the 'inside' they occur once a month. At that moment, I did not take note of 'inside' versus 'outside'. I eventually realized that when the woman said 'inside' she meant inside Green Haven Correctional Facility, a maximum security prison. Really? Was the information worth going into a maximum security prison for? What are the risks? What types of people are there? What had they done to spend their sentence at a maximum security prison?

It did not take me long to decide to go into Green Haven. I could obtain all of this amazing information in a shorter amount of time. I was eager to learn and to start working with youth. I started the process of becoming a volunteer in the prison since this was the only way I could go 'inside'. I was so thankful that although I had gone through my wild days as a youth, I had never put my reputation or future in jeopardy. The paperwork was a breeze.

Then the big day came! I left my house that morning extremely anxious and yet excited. As I sat in my car in front of the immense concrete walls and enormous gate, overwhelmed and a bit dazed, again thought to myself "is it worth it"? The Holy Spirit said to me "you better believe it is worth it" and so I proceeded to the front gate. In order to go inside, I had to remove my belt and shoes and be subjected to a pat down. Humiliating, but necessary I suppose. During orientation a woman proceeded to scare the life out of me. She explained the rules: you cannot talk to any of the inmates for too long because the others will get jealous; you cannot touch the inmates; you cannot take mail from them to be mailed on the outside. She expressed that because I was a muscular guy there would be a few guys that may find me attractive so be aware. Aware?!? I will be alert and ready to get out of there. She told me horror stories about people who did not comply with the rules. If the barrage of intimidating rules alone wasn't enough, she asked me if I was ready to go to the workshop. I have to admit that at that point what I really wanted to do was get out of there and go back home. But the Holy Spirit did it again and said that I had nothing to fear, I had come this far. Of course, I obeyed.

I was escorted from where the orientation took place to a small room where the inmates were setting up the workshop. I was asked to have a seat with the inmates. What am I doing here? Can I turn back now? Some of the inmates approached me, cordially and invitingly and tried to shake my hand. Since the woman at volunteer services had already put fear into me, I pulled my hand back nervously. The guys looked at me like I was crazy! The workshop thankfully started. Early in the morning session, after having awesome conversations with some of the inmates, I simply had to stop the workshop. I openly apologized to the group. I explained what was shared with me at orientation and hoped they would forgive me for my unfriendly behavior. I wanted to start the morning all over. They were not these daunting monsters. They were simply men like me who had made some poor decisions in their lives. They may not have had good mentors or a support system to guide them differently. I was feeling so blessed and could not wait to share this feeling with some of those people who had been so instrumental in shaping my young life.

My admission changed the climate in the room. Not only did I feel better, but it appeared that the inmates became more comfortable and relaxed. Periodically the Corrections Officer would come in to the room to do a count of the inmates. He kept having a miscount, over by one person. Are you serious? They counted me in each time. Inmates there wear green. I did not have on even a stitch of green. What they did see was an African American face...must be an inmate! This hurts me to the core. Was it more hurtful that I was lumped into this group of men spending their lifetime in prison or was it that I was part of a group that stereotypically was finding themselves in this position? Unfortunately, this was not the first time I had experienced this type of discrimination. I just knew that I could be a part of changing this mentality towards African Americans as well as the sad yet true statistic. I just didn't know how at the time.

The weekend was spectacular! Over the course of the thirty hours I spent in Green Haven, I listened as these inmates shared their inner most feelings, the reasons why they were incarcerated, and the troubled past that led them here. Sunday came and while I was driving to the facility for the last day, I was a mess! I thought about leaving later on, heading home to my young wife, and about this amazing experience. The men who I had just bonded with will remain there, some for the rest of their lives. Many of these young men were my age. I was not a saint growing up and probably was moving in the same circles as some of them, yet I was on the outside. Why was I blessed enough to be living my life every day a free man? On this ride in I cried, thankful that God's plan for my life did not include incarceration. I made some true friends that weekend and learned how to be a blessing to young people to ensure that they do not make the same decisions and bad choices, the consequences of which can be life changing.

I started to attend AVP workshops at Green Haven every month. I couldn't get enough of the incredible stories and life altering experiences. I thought about what I had learned constantly and started using some of the activities with the youth groups I worked with. It was incredible how quickly the kids responded; it was as if they were hungry to share the stories of their young lives with me. How could I reach the largest number of students with this life changing experience? I needed to ensure the young people I worked with made good decisions, had a solid foundation including positive feedback and a good mentor. How was I going to accomplish all of this while working for a social work agency? I prayed. My heart was so exposed to each and every young person I met, I could not pass up the opportunity to steer them down the right path. Rachel and I began to talk about it. As we have done so many times before and since then, she and I sat at the kitchen table and brain stormed. This always seems to be the place where we solve the world's problems and encourage one another. Rachel has a gift of taking my words, my fragmented thoughts and phrases and turning them into something substantial. Sitting there one evening at our kitchen table, we drafted a business plan that would guild our lives down an amazing path. Of course, I know this was the path that God had been preparing me for all of my life.

Buckle Up!

GOD HAD PLACED PASSION IN MY HEART to help young people understand life, responsibilities and challenges and to provide them with the necessary tools to succeed and make a positive impact. This passion became my mission. I used all that I had learned from the inmates including their life lessons and designed a succession of experiential workshops that I called Power of Peace. The purpose was to enable young people to become skilled at, experience and apply the knowledge of resolving conflicts, understanding and compassion, teamwork and cooperation and respect for diversity so that their schools and communities would be safer and more productive places for themselves and their peers. I took my passion and mission seriously yet I still did not know what God's plan was for me.

The executive director of the agency where I was working at the time was very impressed with the work I was doing with the youth and believed that there truly was a market, and of course, funding for a program offering these character building components. She began to proactively seek any source of funding to support my efforts and was relatively successful. We received several small grants and the generous support of a donor that was willing to help programs that support youth. But was this where I was supposed to be? Is this where God had planned for me to be using the Gifts that He had given me? I was itching to do more, to be on my own. As He always does, He knew the longings of my heart. I prayed for Him to guide me while I continued to develop the program. It was my supervisor's desire to increase the funding coming in to our agency, seeing my program as the perfect vehicle to do this. What she did not know was that my prayers were about to be answered!

She invited me to a luncheon where she wanted me to dazzle our benefactor with the amazing results of the program I was developing and to encourage her to increase her support. The Holy Spirit was with me during the entire lunch, giving me confidence and guidance. At long last it was my turn to dazzle her! My heart was racing as I crumpled the short speech I had written including several accolades about the program. It just did not seem right! I decided to step out in faith and share with the group that her "money will be safe with me because everything that I do revolves around my Christian principles and I follow the promptings of the Holy Spirit. I don't do any of this work for myself or for the agency but for the glory of God". The Holy Spirit continued to encourage me even though I saw the face of the woman's attorney change to a deep shade of red. I was about to be fired! I stepped out in faith, embarrassed the agency by talking about religion and they were going to fire me. What had I done! When my supervisor stepped away from the table, in my mind clearly to get ready to fire me, the attorney, chuckling, leaned over to me. He said, "You know she is a devoted Christian. We were just discussing on the way over here that she is looking for a program founded on Christian principles". She could not have been more thrilled with my admission – a sigh of relief!

The others at the table now were invisible to me. The conversation turned to faith, church, and beliefs. It was amazing that our prayers had collided at this strange luncheon. Then again God does not do anything by mistake. This initial conversation led to more meals together, not including my coworkers from the agency. At one memorable breakfast meeting with this amazing woman, I decided to ask her if she would consider supporting me directly if I left the agency and ventured out on my own. After careful consideration, she gave me the shock of my life – she said 'yes'! A prominent business man was at this breakfast with me and gave me some words of wisdom as I started to back pedal in fear…"if you turn down this amazing opportunity, what will you tell your kids some day?" It was clear to me that I had just set a new course for my life.

Now what do we do? I had no idea where to start or what to do at this point. I was in a state of shock and again turned to God for my strength. I prayed for His guidance and direction. I can interact with teenagers all day, every day. I knew that my program and methodology were good. Figure out how to start a business? Not my specialty. Rachel, on the other hand, is the resourceful one. She quickly took the rough business plan that we had sketched out at the dinner table and got to researching. Within a few short weeks, we had developed a plan, incorporated as a business and were established as a fully functioning non-profit organization – God is Good! Rachel and I were both in disbelief that I had actually taken this leap of faith and left my comfortable job to start this organization but we knew that it had the Lord's signature and blessing on it.

It has been five years now since we started Youth Voices Center, Inc. and in that time we have reached more than six thousand young people. What an amazing feeling to know that I go to work each and every day and have the possibility of changing someone's life. Passion for the youth I work with resonates from every part of me. If even it is just one student out of a group of twenty five, I know I have impacted the world and made it a better place. As difficult as the non-profit world can be, my angel investor has given me the vehicle that I know is God's will and plan for my life. This amazing woman's faith in God and in me has brought joy to so many young people. I have countless stories of young people faced with unspeakable circumstances in their young lives, yet they have found the strength to go on…the sixteen year old girl being raped by her stepfather and his friends; the gang inductee being forced to violence to become a member; the young girl from an affluent family, longing just to be loved. These kids come to me from all walks of life, all colors and religions yet they all struggle with self-esteem issues, diversity and stereotyping challenges, bullying and an array of pressures and influences. My experiences with the inmates at Green Haven provided me with the idea and tools to help young people become active, productive members of society. It was God's hand on my heart that gave me the passion and motivation to do so.

Why Me?

HAVING BROKEN MY ANKLE during two consecutive seasons playing college football, it was no big surprise to me when I started limping slightly. It was as if arthritis was settling in already. I was only about thirty at the time. Rachel and I were on a vacation in the Bahamas with her family when while on the golf course, I felt a weird pop and fell to the ground. This was the first of many such adventures ending with me on the ground. When we returned home, we went to the doctor but there didn't seem to be anything wrong. Just a strange fall! Why me?

Body building was at the time my sport of choice, replacing football. My weight fluctuated between one hundred ninety eight and two hundred fifty lbs. I noticed my calves looked atrophied sometimes but I didn't think anything other than 'I hadn't worked hard enough' or 'my ankle must be messing with it'. Since weight lifting had been such a large part of my life as a teen thanks to my oldest brother, it was only natural for me to progress into bodybuilding as I got older. I loved it. I am extremely goal oriented and driven, two traits necessary to keep me focused and diligent with my training and which will prove to be life-saving in the future. I continued to work out and exercise and work out some more. Rachel and I met in a gym and we were workout partners for years until she gave birth to our first child, Gabriella.

Even though I continued my intense workout routine, my limp became more and more pronounced. I was losing mobility in my ankle, it became stiffer and stretching did not seem to help. I could stretch and my legs would be just as stiff an hour later. A friend of mine from the gym recommended I see a chiropractor. My IT band was tight, he stretched me, gave me orthotics for my shoes, and stretched me some more. With the birth of our second child, Jaden, time became more precious and scarce. I stopped bodybuilding, but continued to passionately and religiously train in the gym. No matter what was going on in our busy lives, I always carved out time to work out, even if that meant getting up at four am to fit it in before going off to work. My limp was getting worse. My right ankle was now completely immobile and I began to swing my leg out to compensate for the lack of dorsiflexion. This was causing more tightness in my legs and even stiffness in my hip. I saw physical therapists, sports therapists, chiropractors and frankly anyone that would see me.

In 2010, Rachel convinced me to see an orthopedic doctor specializing in sports related injuries. After reviewing my x-rays and doing some tests, he determined that there was "nothing" wrong with my ankle. NOTHING! No arthritis, no bone fragments, no scar tissue…however, he measured it at five percent mobility. Why me? He recommended that I use a device to stretch my Achilles and see what it could do. I spent my entire summer on the couch with this contraption on my leg, thinking it was doing something, making improvements. Yet, in fact, my limp continued to get worse. Not only was I now limping but my balance was off as well. Rachel and the kids would tease about not getting in front of daddy so as not to trip him; we repaired the wall when I fell and put my elbow through it; I tripped down an embankment while out with friends; and I couldn't even maneuver down a grassy slope at the soccer field. It was funny, we laughed and joked but, all along I was praying to God for a miracle. I made excuses why I would not go on weekend adventures or vacation outings with Rachel and the kids. It was difficult for Rachel to be compassionate because she had never experienced anything debilitating. She wanted me to do things with the kids and do normal family things. I was becoming more conscious of my inabilities and disability, especially as more people noticed the limp. It was amazing to me that complete strangers thought it acceptable to comment on my limp. They would stare and ask "what happened to your leg?" My first reaction to this was always, "hi, my name is Mike". Why me? Despite the limp, I was still able to continue my daily workout routine – walking on the treadmill, riding a spin bike and of course, lifting weights. God had created me with this drive, passion, diligence and persistence. I could not let him down.

I continued to study. As I grew closer to God, I tried to accept that maybe this was the path that God wanted me to go down. I would not be able to coach Gabbi's soccer team or show Jaden how to run football plays. Rachel loves to dance and is always the first one on the dance floor no matter the music; I could not get out there with her like I used to. If it wasn't for my faith, I am certain these things could have taken me into a downward spiral of depression. I could not see at the time that there was something, anything for that matter, for me in the future. In the words of Bishop T.D. Jakes, "forsake your comfort to attain your destiny". Really? I have to give up my mobility to reach my goals? Why me?

By the fall of 2011, I was falling all of the time, and was clearly struggling to walk. I continued to believe that my previously broken ankle was the cause of my problems, even though somewhere deep in my heart I was wondering if it wasn't something more. My prayers every day were for deliverance. I asked the Lord to deliver me from this restrictive life and to give me back the things I was missing. As I put on my shield of armor (faith) every day, I asked God to pour down a blessing on me. I was desperate. Rachel suggested that we see another kind of doctor, a podiatrist. She found the best doctor in this area. The next few months of our lives began to swirl like a tornado brewing off in the distance.

Just before Thanksgiving, I went to see the podiatrist. Without even examining my foot or ankle, he told me that I needed to see a neurologist and even called someone across town to make an appointment for me the very same day. It was a few days later when I met with the neurologist, a very capable doctor who immediately scheduled me for an MRI. His words to me will resonate with me forever. "You have either multiple sclerosis or a tumor in your back". Tumor?!? Multiple Sclerosis?!? I was praying for deliverance and what I was getting was an unwelcomed answer. As I cried on my way home, I called Rachel at work to break the news. It was devastating. She told me later that the first thing she did was get on her knees right there in her office and prayed that it was NOT multiple sclerosis. She knew what kind of life that could be for me and for the family. Being the planner in the family, she immediately thought about selling the house and cars for more "handicap" friendly accommodations and transportation. She was thinking about how in the past ten or so years, she had seen me go from a strong athlete to possibly being wheelchair bound with a shortened life expectancy. It was a painful and harsh reality that we both had to face. We were both scared to death but decided not to say anything to our family or friends yet until we knew for sure. We told the kids, four and seven at the time, we were going to doctors to make daddy's leg better.

After three hours inside an MRI machine, I was pretty much freaked out. Picture this…a two hundred and fifty lb. former bodybuilder stuffed inside a small tube. It must have been comical for anyone watching the technicians trying to stuff me inside the machine. I was shaking and swore I would NEVER get in one of those again…until we walked in the front door of our home and the phone rang. "I'm sorry Mr. Arterberry, the radiologist would like to see one more picture, and you will need to come back tomorrow". Dread, fear, aggravation! Why me? Yet I knew this was the key to determining my fate. Of course, we prayed.

After the second day of testing, we went directly to our appointment at the neurologist's office. I have great respect for this doctor and appreciated his frank response to us. It was not multiple sclerosis or a tumor. What a relief! However, he had never seen this before. From his evaluation and review with the radiologist, it was determined that I had either a cyst compressing my spinal cord or a rare phenomenon of a herniated spinal cord. In either case, surgery would be required. How was this possible? I was praying for a miracle, deliverance, I was expecting to wake up one day and be healed. I was not prepared for this news. The doctor admitted he would not be able to treat me but referred us to a colleague at Columbia University Medical Center in Manhattan. How amazing is God…putting all of these people in my path, making it "easy" if such a thing exists in a case like this. All Rachel and I had to do was show up to these appointments, the doctors had arranged for everything else.

We drove in silence to the city that morning in December. We did not know what to say to each other let alone did we want to discuss what may be lying ahead. Not knowing exactly where to go, we parked at a lot at the corner of the block. Unfortunately, the office was at the top of the block up a long hill. This had to be the longest, most difficult walk of my life if you could call it that. It was more of a slow crawl through the cold. I should have had Rachel drop me off. I couldn't complain, or even be angry. I just prayed for good news.

The entrance to the building was full of other people coming and going to their doctor appointments; a lonely place, void of any emotion. I am surprised I even noticed the other people in the elevator; my heart was pounding so hard that it was all I could hear. We were quickly escorted from the waiting room to the doctor's office where a young doctor soon met us. Could he really be the one that was going to "heal" me? Had God given him some amazing powers at such a young age to help me when no one else seems to want to touch me? He was the Director of Minimally Invasive Surgery at one of the most well-known hospitals in the country. This had God's hand all over it.

After a few quick tests and watching my belabored gait, the doctor asked Rachel and I to join him in his office. He was very serious, but then again, how should he be? He confirmed that either I had a cyst compressing my spinal cord or a herniated spinal cord as the others had suspected. He recommended surgery. "Not a chance" I thought. There is no way that he is going to cut me open. I realize that I had been asking for a miracle but this is NOT it.

Rachel tried to be comforting as I threw out lame excuses about work. She suggested that maybe I could wait until the summer when work was typically slower. The doctor never changed his demeanor when he said sternly that this surgery could not wait, we had to do it right away. I guess neither one of us had yet fully understood what he was talking about. It was not until we talked about it that we realized that due to the duration and the lack of spinal fluid flowing to my lower extremities, I was slowly being paralyzed. The nerves in my feet and ankles were dying and unless I did something about it, my legs would too. He could not in fact believe that I was able to walk into his office and even able to lift weights. Could I really wake up one morning and not be able to walk at all? Why me? This was his fear and possibly my reality. My first question was "will I be back to normal"? Again, in his unchanging, emotionless way, the doctor informed me that I 'may' be back to where I am now after surgery but there is no way to repair a spinal cord. I was in complete disbelief. Now I REALLY wasn't doing the surgery....why would I let them cut me open just to be where I am today, limping, dragging my leg, not being able to run and play with the kids. I would take my chances.

During the long ride out of the city, Rachel and I spoke only briefly about it. In her mind, I had to have the surgery without a doubt. I was still determined that I was not doing it. I needed guidance…my first phone call was to my pastor, my friend. I just needed to speak to him. I drove to the church as soon as I could. After hearing the entire scenario, he agreed. I would be crazy to let them cut me open. I wanted to believe that God would let me wake up tomorrow morning and I would miraculously be healed. I needed to believe this. Unbeknownst to me, Rachel was terrified. How could this be happening? We were both in a stupor, not emotional, or crying, just numb. We tried not to discuss it much in front of the kids, so as not to alarm them. I called my brother who has usually given me good advice over the years. I was hoping he would be supportive and he too agreed that I should not have the surgery.

The very next day Rachel called a college friend of hers who is a physical therapist. She told her everything we had heard and asked her to explain it in laymen's terms. Her first question to Rachel was "when is the surgery scheduled?" She didn't bat an eye. There was not a shadow of a doubt in her mind that I had to have the surgery and soon. Rachel immediately called me with the information she had just received from her friend. She trusted her and knew that she had an infinite amount of information compared to what we knew – nothing! As soon as I heard her comments, I was convinced and we started the next phase. We contacted another well-known hospital that specializes in this type of surgery for a second opinion. We called the doctor in Manhattan to proceed and determine the battery of additional tests we would need to do. Yet, I still had this burning question: how much mobility would I get back? Will I walk "normal" again? I asked everyone. I mean "everyone". While I was in the hospital having more tests done, I asked the x-ray technician, the radiologist, even the young man who moved the gurney from one room to the next. I just needed to know. Finally, Rachel asked 'how many more people are you going to ask the same question and expect a different answer? Who will you ask next, the janitor?" I was hoping to hear just one person tell me what I wanted to hear...I would have a full recovery and run like I used to. I was an athlete all my life and now I could barely make it to the bathroom without struggling. I had to have faith but honestly, my faith was shaken and fragile. I needed to trust God more than ever right now but instead, I was relying on a person to tell me my fate. Why was it so hard to just believe and have Faith that God would deliver me? Why me? It was not the way I expected to be healed but, maybe this was God's way.

January 27th, 2012. It was three am and Rachel and I were in the car on our way to pick up my mother. She needed to be there with her youngest son as he underwent this very dangerous, very serious surgery to repair his spinal cord. I needed her there. Rachel needed her there. Even though she had been so strong, so logical, so faithful the past few months since I first saw the podiatrist, Rachel was unsure if she could be at the hospital alone all day, just waiting. It has taken Rachel many years to draw close to God and develop a relationship with Him. I now saw how she has grown and was relying on Him. I needed her at this moment to be my rock since my own faith, faith that I have proudly worn on my sleeve for years, faith that has carried me through all of the peaks and valleys before, was now under attack. I screamed out to God, "Help".

Since the tests had not conclusively determined exactly what procedure was to be done, the doctors prepared for the more difficult of the two: the herniated spinal cord. If this was the case, the doctors expected to have to scrape bone and implant hardware to reposition my spinal cord, an innovative doctor's dream surgery. My worst nightmare.... why me? As the three of us arrived at the hospital early that morning, we could not believe our eyes. Dozens of other people there at five thirty in the morning to have some type of procedure. What was their condition? What about their belief in God? Did they know that if something happened to them that day that they would go to heaven? Did they trust God or were they putting blind faith in the hands of the very skilled and talented yet very human doctors? As I prayed for myself, I also had to say a prayer for all of the people around me, praying that we would all make it home to our families.

After the admission process, I was promptly escorted to a preoperative area where they began to hook me up to machines and poke me with needles. Although I have never had high blood pressure before, it was very elevated this morning. I was so nervous, terrified actually. Before Jaden and Gabbi left the night before with my mother-in-law, we talked about what was going to happen to daddy. Bless Jaden's little heart. At four years old, the wonderful thought he left with was that daddy was going to 'make dust' behind him when he runs so fast after the doctor's fix his leg. In his world, he was going to have a great weekend with Gramme and then run with daddy in a few days. Making dust has become our family's way of describing someone or something running really fast. I wish I could see it all from a child's eyes.

I was soon taken into the operative area where they gave me gowns and booties. Imagine the sight...this big man wearing one small gown facing forward and another backward, pants that were too small and little booties on his feet. My doctor came in to do a quick evaluation of me and still couldn't believe that I was walking. I didn't really call it that these days but he was surprised nevertheless. All I kept thinking was 'please let me go to the bathroom before I go in there'. God knows my bladder will not hold up for very long, another symptom of a spinal cord issue. I said goodbye to Rachel and my mom and I 'walked' off to the operating room. Why me?

My prayer partners waited patiently. They prayed. They talked. As awful as the circumstances were, it was a wonderful bonding experience for the two of them. Rachel knows that she could not possibly have sat there all day without my mom, anxiously waiting for some news. As they prayed for the best, they felt blessed. How could that be? I was in God's hands, with a skilled team of surgeons. The family sitting next to them had been awakened in the middle of the night by a call telling them to be at the hospital immediately for the father to receive a new heart….Rachel described it as a sickening feeling to know that this man was getting a new heart right now because someone else had just died. We are blessed!

It was a very long day. The hours passed and no news yet. The doctors had originally said that it would take five hours or so if it was the cyst and seven hours or more if it was the herniated spinal cord. After seven hours, Rachel and my mom began to get worried. Finally, my doctor arrived with a huge smile on his face. Everything had gone well and they could see me soon.

Waking up in the recovery room I was dazed, delirious and drugged. I had this amazing rushing sensation as I could only imagine was spinal fluid freely flowing to my legs and feet. I had feeling in my toes – I didn't even know that I had lost it. I could move my ankles, my toes. My legs felt "lighter". All of these years, the slow progression of the compression, I didn't realize how much sensation I had been losing. Now to feel this rushing – was it really happening or just my desire to feel it? The doctor came in and his words were music to my ears, "It was just a cyst"- God is Good! Amazing! I shouted and danced inside, praising God at the top of my lungs. My soul rejoiced as I heard these words and I just couldn't contain my elation. Every nurse, doctor and visitor in the recovery room could hear my praises. I think I bordered on preaching. I am certain everyone was laughing at my outlandish shouts of joy and excitement.

I know that the location of the cyst only impacted my lower extremities. I believe my surgeon was the best in the field, very competent, and knowledgeable. But, he couldn't explain to me why I had this warm feeling in my right hand. It was suddenly warm, almost sweaty as I laid there in the recovery room. Nothing my doctors had done would scientifically explain it. It wasn't until several days later that I fully understood....

God was Holding my Hand!

My hand returned to being slightly cold all of the time. No one is quite sure why this is. I am ok with it because I now know without a shadow of a doubt that God was with me that day as he has been during all of those critical times in my life. He walks with me always and if I look back, I am certain I would see a second pair of footprints in the sand. He has a plan for my life. My family, sports, my Christian walk, the youth program, surgery…all part of God's plan.

I try to be a blessing to everyone that I cross paths with in my life; to demonstrate how as a Christian we should walk, to be like Jesus. I hope that my testimony, how God always makes a way, is always there and lets us go through things so we can be that light shining on his goodness, can be a message to someone. Don't give up hope; God always has a Divine plan and purpose for your life. We may not understand or appreciate the hardships but there is always a plan. God loves me, He loves all of us…we may not know what His plan is, but it is coming. Buckle Up!

House where I grew up, condemned after we moved out.

Middle school football.

College football.

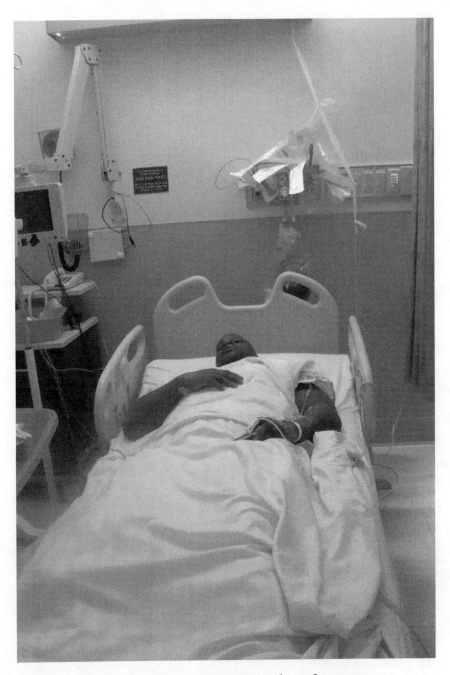

Just hours after having spinal cord surgery.

Update

IT HAS BEEN A LONG SLOW RECOVERY, but God is Good and keeps his promises. I had to have faith that He does miracles. I was looking for an instant miracle and was eager for the doctors to tell me that I would walk normal again. Had I simply relied on the word of God as my guide all along, I would have known that he would restore me and use me as a testimony to his goodness. In the midst of it all, I could not see God's plan. Nearly nine months later I have made dramatic improvements in all areas of my physical health. My limp has drastically diminished and I can do things I could never do before. Most people, including my neurosurgeon, would not recognize me from the man I was before my journey.

Have faith that God has a plan for your life. You are uniquely and specifically created with a plan. It may not be the plan of your choosing, but trust that God will reveal his plan and purpose to you.

References

Carle, Eric "The Very Hungry Caterpillar"
   1987 Penguin Putnam Books

Jakes, Bishop T.D. June 27, 2012 message

Resources

Alternatives to Violence Project/New York State
   http://avpny.org/

Youth Voices Center, Inc.
   http://www.youthvoicescenter.org/

Made in the USA
San Bernardino, CA
04 December 2012